Original title:
In the Spirit of Christmas Wonder

Copyright © 2024 Creative Arts Management OÜ
All rights reserved.

Author: Clara Whitfield
ISBN HARDBACK: 978-9916-90-980-5
ISBN PAPERBACK: 978-9916-90-981-2

A Canvas of White

The snow fell down without a care,
Turning streets into fluffy chairs.
Kids in jackets, sleds in tow,
Face first in snowdrifts, oh what a show!

Snowmen with hats and carrot noses,
Slipping and sliding, oh, the poses!
Winter wonderland, a snowy plight,
Let's make hot cocoa, then take a bite!

Carols in the Air

Singing loud, voices off-key,
Gift exchanges near the tree.
Santa's sleigh stuck in a jam,
Rudolph's nose? It's just a flan!

Elf on a shelf, what a view,
Peeking at cookies, and milk too.
Jingle bells ringing in the night,
Dance like no one's in your sight!

The Warmth of Togetherness

Gather 'round for a feast of fun,
Turkey's cooking, oh what a run!
Grandma's pie, so rich and sweet,
Watch your waistline, now take a seat!

Laughter echoes, stories to share,
Falling off chairs? You better beware!
Family's close, but jokes fly high,
Who dropped the turkey? Oh, my oh my!

Starlit Wishes

Under stars that wink and gleam,
Wishing on jokes, not just a dream.
Fireflies buzzing, what a delight,
Moon's dancing, oh what a sight!

Whispers of secrets float in the air,
Stargazing, giggles, without a care.
Let's make a wish for silly things,
Like flying pigs with sparkly wings!

Pinecone Dreams and Sugarplum Nights

In a forest full of pine,
I dreamed of cakes and wine.
The squirrels danced in delight,
While snowflakes started their flight.

Sugarplums bounced from tree to tree,
Singing sweet songs just for me.
Their giggles filled the winter air,
As I tried to join their bear fair.

Oh, to twirl like a sugar sprite,
On this whimsical, starry night.
With pinecone crowns upon our heads,
We'll snack on dreams and cozy beds.

So come and prance to this fun tune,
Underneath the big bright moon.
We'll laugh and glide in goofy ways,
In pinecone dreams and sugarplum plays.

Emblems of Togetherness and Peace

Two socks lost in the wash,
Wonder where they go, oh gosh!
They're off to dance a merry jig,
While I sit here, pulling my big wig.

A cat and dog share a bowl,
Chasing each other, that's their goal.
With tails that twirl and eyes so bright,
They'll make peace over a midnight bite.

Friends gather round with treats in hand,
Sharing stories that are quite unplanned.
With laughter flowing strong and loud,
Creating memories, we feel so proud.

So raise a toast to those near and far,
To the silly moments, that's who we are.
In the spirit of joy, let's take a chance,
And celebrate our quirkiest dance.

Dancing Flames and Cozy Moments

The fire crackles, pops, and glows,
While marshmallows dance in fiery throws.
We poke and prod with sticks in hand,
Creating gooey sweets that are simply grand.

In cozy chairs, we share our dreams,
With shadows casting funny schemes.
The flames flicker, our faces bright,
In warmth and laughter, we'll spend the night.

A mug of hot cocoa to warm our toes,
While stories flow like melting snores.
Each giggle bubbling up like a stream,
In the glow of the fire, we find our gleam.

So let's embrace this lovely scene,
With dancing flames that feel so keen.
As moments cozy, friends unite,
In this joyful, starry night.

Tinsel Trails and Golden Hues

Tinsel trails across the floor,
Just like confetti, who could ask for more?
The cat jumps in, oh what a sight,
Riding the waves of sparkling light.

Golden hues upon the tree,
Reflecting dreams of you and me.
Ornaments made from a silly mood,
Dancing the night in festive food.

Eggnog spills on the table spread,
As laughter fills our merry shed.
With games that make no quiet time,
We'll jingle all the way in rhyme!

So join the fun, let's celebrate,
With tinsel dreams on our plate.
In a merry dance of joy and cheer,
We'll share our hearts, and toast the year.

Whispers of Winter's Magic

Snowflakes dance with glee,
While squirrels sip their tea.
Frosty noses, chilly toes,
Winter's winks, nobody knows.

Hot cocoa's got a mustache,
While penguins start to splash.
Snowmen smile, their eyes of coal,
Hoping for a snowball roll.

The fireplace cracks a joke,
As weaves the woolly cloak.
Chatter, laughter fills the air,
While frosty doom, we don't care.

In winter's whimsy, we delight,
Chasing snowflakes, pure delight.
Though frozen, warm hearts stay,
In this wild, winter play.

Lanterns in the Snow

Lanterns twinkle, snowflakes soar,
Kids with snowballs plot and score.
The wind howls, a ghostly tune,
While cats chase shadows beneath the moon.

The snowman wears a funky hat,
With carrots lost, where's his snack?
A cat called Whiskers takes a leap,
Into snowdrifts, oh so deep.

Lights are strung with care and flair,
But tangled up, we pull our hair.
Sleds go zooming, whoosh and squeal,
As laughter echoes, oh, what a deal!

All around the world's aglow,
In that chilly winter show.
With lanterns bright, we stomp and play,
Creating magic, come what may.

Echoes of Joyful Hearts

Laughter rings like silver bells,
In cozy nooks where friendship dwells.
Gobbling treats, we make a mess,
But oh, the joy, we must confess!

Chasing shadows, playing games,
Every friend shouts out their names.
Messy hair and frosty cheeks,
The magic's found in joyful peaks.

Sledding down the hilly slopes,
Crafting dreams, and building hopes.
When snowmen frown, we just can't stop,
With giggles loud, we jump, we hop!

So gather round, warm hearts unite,
In wintersweet, we find pure light.
As echoes dance upon the air,
We freeze in time, without a care.

A Tapestry of Twinkling Lights

Strings of lights in every tree,
Sparking joy, oh can't you see?
Frosty fairies dance around,
In this winter wonderland found.

Mittens lost and hats askew,
As snowflakes fall, we all pursue.
The dog digs deep for a bone,
While laughter echoes, oh so grown!

Baking cookies, what a treat,
With sprinkles, icing—all things sweet.
Yet somehow flour fills the air,
Snowy mess! But who will care?

A tapestry of cheer and glow,
In each heart, the warm winds blow.
So let's embrace this winter's night,
With twinkling lights, it feels so right.

Once Upon a Frosty Night

Once upon a frosty night,
A penguin danced in furry tights.
He slipped and slid, began to prance,
In search of snacks, he found romance.

The snowflakes fell like popcorn bright,
While snowmen had a snowball fight.
But one went rogue, and what a sight,
He chased a dog, oh what a fright!

A reindeer lost his way, it seems,
He mistook a tree for ice cream dreams.
With every scoop, he gained a cheer,
But all he got was frozen beer.

So laughter rang across the night,
With every slip and snowy bite.
And if you ask the penguin now,
He'll say, "Worst date! But hey, wow!"

The Warm Embrace of Giving

A box of socks, a silly gift,
To make your feet do a happy lift.
Wrapped in bows and shiny paper,
They smell like cheese, but that's a caper.

A hat so bright, it blinds the sun,
With pompons so big, it's just plain fun.
Yet who would wear such wacky glory?
The neighbor's cat, in all its story.

A fruitcake served, all boxed and tied,
With nuts and raisins stacked inside.
One bite and you'll make a face,
But hey! That's how we share our grace!

So give a gift, embrace the cheer,
Even if it's filled with fear.
And if they laugh, just take a bow,
For giving joy is what you vow!

Nightfall's Serenade of Hope

As night descends, the stars do gleam,
While raccoons plot their midnight dream.
They gather snacks, a feast in glee,
With pizza crusts and cola tea.

The moon peeks through the shady trees,
Where owls discuss the latest breeze.
They hoot about their night-time spree,
While foxes sing just to be free.

A cat composed a midnight tune,
With scrappy lyrics, under the moon.
It serenades the sleepy streets,
While chasing tails and dancing feet.

With every note, a spark of jest,
They celebrate the silly quest.
So as you drift into your sleep,
Remember, dreams are yours to keep!

Glimmers of Laughter in the Hearth

The fireplace crackles, bright and bold,
While marshmallows toast, their tales unfold.
A squirrel steals cookies, what a thief!
While grandpa's jokes bring joy and grief.

The stockings hang with care tonight,
But one fell down, oh what a sight!
It swallowed toys, a teddy bear,
And made a home, a cozy lair.

As laughter fills the chilly room,
The cat rehearses for its doom.
From the chimney comes a smoky plume,
While kids dance round, creating gloom.

So gather 'round, let joy take flight,
In the glimmers of this warm delight.
For in this hearth, hearts ignite,
In laughter's glow, the world feels right!

The Heart's Radiance

A heart so bright it lights the room,
Yet sometimes slips and causes gloom.
It dances here, it trips on toes,
Then giggles at the mess it sows.

With every beat, it sings a song,
Of love that's right and just so wrong.
Like ice cream cones that melt too fast,
Or silly jokes that never last.

It beams like sun through cloudy skies,
Yet just as often wears a disguise.
With friends, it sparkles like the bling,
But trips on thoughts of avocado spring.

So when you see that radiant glow,
Laugh with the heart, let good vibes flow.
For every blunder, every cheer,
Makes life's sweet symphony sincere.

Kindness Wrapped in Warmth

A hug so tight, it's like a quilt,
It warms your heart, makes worries melt.
It sprinkles smiles and dashes cheer,
Like lemonade in summer's sphere.

With laughter that could light a fire,
It lifts you up and takes you higher.
It bakes you cookies, shares a seat,
And dances with you to a funky beat.

Kindness wrapped in warmth, a gift,
In cozy moments, hearts do lift.
Like fluffy socks on winter days,
Or silly hats in funny ways.

So share some love, don't you delay,
In this crazy world, make kindness stay.
For warmth and joy are what we crave,
In life's big sea, let's be the wave.

The Melody of Merriment

A tune so bright, it makes you sway,
With happy thoughts that shout hooray!
It jingles like a bell on bikes,
And tickles noses just like spikes.

With laughter sprouting with each note,
It dances 'round like a silly goat.
A melody that stirs the heart,
And makes you feel the joyful art.

From rolls of laughter to silly games,
It's like a circus with no claims.
Balloons and cakes, confetti flies,
It paints the world in vibrant skies.

So let this melody take a chance,
And whirl you off in a merry dance.
For life is better with a tune,
That makes us laugh beneath the moon.

Snowy Serenity

A blanket white that hushes sound,
Where laughter echoes all around.
With snowflakes tumbling, soft and light,
It wraps the world in pure delight.

In boots that slip and sleds that glide,
We build our forts and take a ride.
With cheeks like cherries, noses red,
And hot cocoa that's sweetly fed.

The trees wear scarves of frosty lace,
While snowmen sport a funny face.
We wander through this winter scene,
In every flake, a spark of dream.

So cherish each snow-drenched day,
With snowy wins and silly play.
In this serene and frosty land,
Find joy in every snowy strand.

Fragrant Pine and Joyful Times

The pine trees smell so nice,
But squirrels think it's their paradise.
They steal our snacks and run away,
Laughing at us every day.

In the forest, we sing loud,
While dancing like a silly crowd.
A bird once joined, forgot the tune,
But swayed as if it was a loon.

With every step, we trip and fall,
The laughter echoes, bounding tall.
Our faces bright with pinecone hats,
We prance around, just like the cats.

As evening falls, the news unfolds,
A raccoon steals the nuts so bold.
We chase it off with gleeful screams,
And now we're just living our dreams.

Gathered Around the Hearth

Gathered 'round in comfy chairs,
We're all Jack Frost's little heirs.
With hot cocoa spilling here,
Our laughter warms the winter cheer.

The fire crackles, pops and glows,
While Uncle Joe recites his prose.
We roll our eyes as he starts to yawn,
And everyone knows he's just a con.

A cat walks by with an air of grace,
And knocks down a mug, oh what a place!
It's all in fun, a little disaster,
We laugh it off and find it faster.

As shadows dance and stories weave,
We're wrapped in joy, I truly believe.
Together here, we face the night,
With hearth and heart, everything's right.

Echoes of Laughter

In a field where daisies sway,
We prance around in bright macaroon play.
With a silly jig and joyful song,
We hop and skip, nothing feels wrong.

A duck quacks back, thinks it's a sage,
Ignoring us fools, on center stage.
We wiggle and giggle, fall on our knees,
The echoing laughter plays in the breeze.

Off to the creek to catch a fish,
But instead, we get quite a squish.
With muddy boots and giggles dear,
Our captures are mainly splashes and cheer.

At dusk we collapse, our energy spent,
Shooting stars above as our laughter's lent.
While echoes ring through the moonlit trees,
We vow to relive these moments with ease.

The Beauty of Togetherness

Together we bake, oh what a sight,
Flour on noses, it's pure delight.
My recipe's gone all upside down,
But we just laugh, wear it like a crown.

The kitchen's chaos, a real true blast,
And the dog thinks it's a feast at last.
With whipped cream fights, how could we stop?
We make a mess that would make mom flop.

A photo op with our messy hair,
We strike a pose, we don't have a care.
This culinary art, so wild and free,
Is just us creating a sweet memory.

In friendship's glow, we find our way,
With laughter and love in each passing day.
The moments we share, oh how they please,
It's the beauty of togetherness with ease.

Unwrapping Joy

Beneath the tree, the gifts abound,
I sniffed a box, and squeaked a sound!
A sweater's in it, oh, what a shame,
It's three sizes too big—who's to blame?

With joy we tear the paper away,
Surprise! Another tie for Uncle Jay!
Everyone laughs, what a funny sight,
At family feasts, no one feels quite right.

The dog's in the mix, unwrapping too,
He found the socks that once were new.
Amid the ruckus, joy fills the air,
Wrapping paper flies, without a care.

So unwrap your smiles, don't stay aloof,
Joy's in the chaos, that's the proof!
With laughter and love, we'll always cheer,
Unwrapping joy, year after year!

The Essence of Togetherness

Gather 'round, let's share our tales,
Of burnt turkey and epic fails.
Together we giggle, together we sip,
From cups that spill, it's a friendship trip!

Cousins conspire with sneaky plans,
To steal the cake from sly little hands.
Siblings argue, over whose turn it is,
To control the remote—what a family biz!

In moments we laugh, in moments we sigh,
A cacophony of voices, oh my, oh my!
With clattering dishes and silly jokes,
We savor the clash of our various folks.

For in this mess, love's the key,
Embracing our quirks, wild and free.
Togetherness shines in every brawl,
A wacky dance routine, we're one and all!

A Glimpse of Magic

In the garden, fairies dance with glee,
I tripped on a toadstool—oh, pardon me!
The kittens wear hats, looking oh so grand,
While squirrels plot cheese thefts, ever so planned.

With a flick of my wand, I order a snack,
But I conjured a pickle—where's the chimichurri at?
Magic can be tricky, as you can see,
It turns my best wishes into goofy decree.

The moon began winking, the stars took a bow,
The cat stalks a shadow, it's magic, wow!
A large rabbit hopped by, with sunglasses on,
"Just out for a stroll, don't mind me," he yawned.

So hold on to laughter, in every slight twist,
For magic is laughter—don't forget this!
With giggles and tricks, life's a bright stage,
A glimpse of the magic is simply the rage!

Frosty Mornings and Cozy Evenings

Frosty mornings bite my nose,
But cocoa warms me to my toes.
I slip on socks, they don't quite match,
In this cozy world, there's no need to hatch.

The snowflakes twirl in wobbly cues,
The dogs are jumping like they've got shoes.
I call my dog, he looks so spry,
But he just wants to chase the sky!

The Magic of Yuletide

A jolly man in a red suit, so bright,
Slides down chimneys, what a silly sight!
He brings us joy and lots of cheer,
But I'm worried that my cat might reappear.

The lights all twinkle, such a pretty show,
Now my house looks like a disco, whoa!
But when I trip on the gift wrap mess,
The magic fades with the slightest stress!

Gifts from the Heart

Gifts from the heart, they say with glee,
But Aunt Edna's socks? Not quite for me!
I'll smile and hug, then swiftly hide,
Those yarn creations, a bumpy ride.

Homemade cookies all laced with love,
Some taste like heaven, some like a shove!
Yet each sweet bite will make me sing,
This holiday cheer is a wondrous thing!

Starry Nights and Silent Snow

Starry nights with a moon so bright,
Make me wish for a snowball fight.
But out I go, I trip and fall,
It seems my coordination's fought with wall!

Silent snowflakes cover my head,
A fat snowman dreams by his bed.
He waves at me with a carrot nose,
But I think he'd prefer to freeze his toes!

Sleigh Bells and Dreaming Pines

Up in the air, those sleighs take flight,
With reindeer dancing, what a sight!
Santa's in trouble, he lost a shoe,
And Rudolph's nose is stuck in glue!

Gifts are clanging, a noisy mess,
Elves are giggling, what a stress!
Jingle bells ringing, a cat's on the roof,
Paws on the shingles, now that's the proof!

Snowflakes are falling, watch out for drifts,
Hope no one slips, or it's "sleigh-tastic" lifts!
Mrs. Claus laughing, with a cookie in hand,
"Watch your step, dear, this wasn't planned!"

So grab your cocoa, let's warm our toes,
With silly sleigh rides and frosty woes!
Dreaming of pines and the sounds of cheer,
What a wild ride this time of year!

Frosted Wishes on Candy Canes

Candy canes twirling in a sugary dance,
Frosted wishes bring a sweet romance!
I tried to build a snowman so grand,
But ended up with a pile of sand!

Minty flavors on a delightful spree,
Wintertime giggles, just you and me.
Sipping hot chocolate, oh what a treat,
But spilled it all over my brand new seat!

Snow angels flapping, in coats that are bright,
The neighborhood cat thinks it's a kite!
Wrapped in layers, we laugh 'til we drop,
'Though my nose is frozen, I'll never stop!

So here's to frosted wishes so sweet,
With candy canes turning our chaos to neat.
In this jolly season, hold laughter tight,
For candy-coated moments shine so bright!

The Gift of Silent Stars

Silent stars shimmer, oh what a show,
While I search for warmth, where did it go?
Beneath all the twinkling, a joke would dwell,
Did I just trip? Oh! On that old, wet shell!

The moon's playing peek-a-boo with the cheeky night,
Wishing for gifts, but I'm out of sight!
A reindeer is dancing, I think he lost track,
Don't blame the cookies, they've got my back!

As I make wishes, out loud I declare,
Dear stars above, do you have a spare?
With giggles and laughter, I float like a kite,
Thanks for the starlight, it's feeling just right!

So here's to a night under starry skies,
Where laughter and wishes are the ultimate prize.
In this cosmic game, we'll all play our part,
The gift of silent stars warms every heart!

Embracing the Chilly Glow

In winter's embrace, a chilly glow,
With snowball fights putting on a show!
Frost-covered cheeks and noses so red,
My hat just flew off; now where's that thread?

Sipping warm cider, what a delight,
But the mug's too hot— oh, what a fright!
The fire is crackling, but so is my hair,
Might need a snowplow to clear out despair!

We build igloos that turn into mush,
"Hey, that's my mitt! Watch out for the rush!"
But laughter, you see, is the best of joy,
Even when winter plays tricks on the boy!

So let's raise a toast to this chilly affair,
With twinkling lights and warmth in the air.
Embracing the glow, with glee and bright cheer,
Wintertime mishaps— they bring us near!

Magical Moments Unfold

A rabbit popped out of my hat,
It looked quite grumpy, imagine that!
Twirling my wand, I made it dance,
It tripped on its ears—what a chance!

The fairy forgot her magic dust,
She spilled some tea, oh what a must!
A gnome in a tutu joined the fun,
They all laughed till the setting sun.

A unicorn slipped on a rainbow slide,
With silly giggles, the fairies cried.
A dragon played tag with a sneaky sprite,
Oh, magical moments, what a delight!

When wands and whims meet in a whirl,
Every day feels like a silly twirl.
So grab your hat, let's make some cheer,
These moments unfold, with friends near!

Love Wrapped in Bows

I wrapped my heart in a big red bow,
But tripped in the yard, oh no, oh no!
The mailman chuckled, he saw it all,
He slipped on my love—oh what a fall!

My cat thought the gift was for her,
As she played with ribbons, that little fur blur.
With hearts and giggles, we danced around,
Wrapping love up as fun was found.

The chocolate melted, hearts went pop,
My sweetheart laughed, we just couldn't stop.
With hugs so tight, and laughter so loud,
Love wrapped in bows makes us so proud.

We share silly jokes, love notes on the way,
Every moment we cherish, come what may.
In each little gift, we see our glow,
Wrapped in affection, love's the best show!

The Wish Upon a Star

I wished for pizza, all loaded and hot,
But got a flying fish, and that was a plot!
It flopped in my lap, with eyes so wide,
I couldn't help laughing, what a silly ride!

The star twinkled back, with a wink and a grin,
Pasta in pools, where do I begin?
A spaghetti monster danced with delight,
In my kitchen, oh what a sight!

I asked for a puppy, sweet, fluffy, and small,
Instead, I got puns that could make you fall.
"Bark-ley and Meowgic" was their clever name,
Oh, wishing on stars is a practical game!

Next time I'll ask for a wondrous treat,
Or a wacky adventure or something to eat.
With giggles and dreams riding high like a car,
Let's keep wishing together—for that's who we are!

Northern Lights and Cozy Nights

The northern lights were dancing bright,
In my backyard, what a cozy sight!
Wrapped in blankets, hot cocoa in hand,
We laughed at the stars, a shimmering band.

The squirrels debated, would it snow?
While snowflakes twirled in the moonlit glow.
With marshmallow snowmen we built with glee,
"They look like us!" shouted, "Can you see?"

The stars had a party on this chilly night,
With comets and giggles, what pure delight!
A penguin slid in, doing a jig,
Then tripped on a snowman—oh, that was big!

So gather 'round friends, with your toes all warm,
Under the sky, hear the weather's charm.
With each cozy moment, laughter takes flight,
Here's to our nights, magical and bright!

Miracles Beneath the Tree

Under the tree, a squirrel grins,
Mixing nuts like he's got wins.
A chipmunk joins, with tiny feet,
Dancing around, a nutty beat.

Leaves fall down like tiny hats,
The birds, they gossip, all like chitchats.
A worm peeks out, says "What a view!"
While ants are marching, in a queue.

Sunshine filters down so bright,
The shadows play, what a sight!
Every creature joins the spree,
In miracles beneath the tree.

A rabbit hops, thinking it's grand,
With a rainbow painted on its hand.
Laughter echoes, all around,
In this happy, silly ground.

A Dance of Hope and Cheer

A twirl of dreams on a sparkly night,
Balloons are floating, what a sight!
The moon's in on this bright charade,
Winking at wishes, unafraid.

Dancing slippers, made of cheese,
Whirling round with all the bees.
A cat joins in with a serenade,
While butterflies play charades.

Joy spills forth in every leap,
With music that makes the sun peep.
Feet tap along; it's quite the show,
In a dance of hope, spirits glow.

So raise your arms to the shining stars,
Let's jive and jig without any scars.
In the wild and wonderful cheer,
We find the magic, always near.

Sparkling Eyes and Innocent Laughter

A puddle splashes, giggles erupt,
Little feet dance, happily corrupt.
With sparkling eyes, they leap and spin,
Chasing rainbows, let the fun begin.

A balloon floats, tied to a dream,
Kids laugh aloud, a joyful scream.
Bubbles rise to tickle the sky,
Each pop a giggle, oh my oh my!

Crafts made of paper, glue all around,
Creating wonders that astound.
With crayons drawn, they color the day,
Innocent laughter, come out and play.

Together they build, a world so bright,
With all the treasures of pure delight.
In their little hearts, joy's a song,
In sparkling eyes, they all belong.

Wishes on the Wind

A dandelion fluff drifts and sways,
Carrying wishes, come what may.
Children point, with hands outstretched,
Chasing dreams, so perfectly etched.

The breeze whispers tales of delight,
As kites flutter high, a colorful flight.
Each gust brings a story anew,
Wrapped in laughter, skies so blue.

A feather floats, light as a thought,
Hope in the air, never caught.
Every whisper, a tiny cheer,
Wishes on the wind, crystal clear.

So toss a coin, watch it gleam,
For every wish is part of the theme.
On this wild ride of whimsy and trends,
Let's sail on laughter, where magic mends.

Rejoicing in the Twinkling Sky

Stars above, oh what a sight,
They twinkle like a disco light.
Dancing jokes in a cosmic show,
As I trip on twinkling snow.

Aliens wave, I think they see,
My hot cocoa and me, it's free!
I raise my mug, they send a wink,
Maybe they also love to drink!

Comets zoom, they flip and dive,
A cosmic giggle keeps me alive.
I ask the moon for a late-night snack,
It throws me cheese from its silver pack!

So let's rejoice in skies so bright,
With laughter, cocoa, and pure delight.
For every twinkle, every gleam,
Is just the universe's silly dream!

Tales from a Winter's Hearth

By the fire, the stories start,
A grumpy cat with a gallant heart.
He guards the socks like they're pure gold,
Only purring when he's told!

A snowman danced, or at least tried,
With carrot nose, he looked so wide.
He slipped and fell, what a loud crash!
Turns out he just loved a good splash!

Hot chocolate spills with a marshmallow poof,
As the dog makes off with my fluffy roof.
Chasing him down, with a laugh and a shout,
Winter's mischief, I can't live without!

So gather 'round, come one, come all,
For tales of laughter, you'll have a ball.
At this winter's hearth, so warm and bright,
The magic is real, up here at night!

Twinkling Lights and Silent Nights

Twinkling lights on every tree,
They blink at me, so joyfully.
I hung them up, then lost my shoe,
Tripped on the tinsel, that's nothing new!

Silent nights, but not my cat,
She's scaling walls, now where's she at?
With a pounce and a leap, she claims her throne,
On the sofa, all cozy alone!

Cookies baked, oh what a mess,
I maybe added too much zest!
The dog now bakes on the kitchen floor,
Who knew he'd love to cook and score?

So here we are, in festive cheer,
With twinkling lights and much love near.
In silent nights, the laughter grows,
As joy and mischief come in glows!

Whispers of Holiday Magic

Whispers dance in the frosty air,
As I scramble to find my favorite chair.
The jingle bells ringing with every cheer,
I misplace my keys, oh dear, oh dear!

There's magic hidden in every hug,
Especially when wrapped in a warm rug.
Elves at work, they seem to grin,
With every mishap, it's a win-win!

The mistletoe sways, oh what a tease,
My cat just jumped, with utmost ease.
He lands right next to the cookies arranged,
And devours them all, highly unchained!

So let the holidays bring forth a laugh,
In every moment, every gaffe.
For magic whispers, this night so bright,
We'll find the joy in holiday light!

Nights of Comfort and Joy

The couch is my throne, it's so plush,
With snacks piled high, I'll never rush.
Pajamas my armor, against the cold,
I'm ready for stories to be told.

A blanket burrito, snug and tight,
Remote in hand, I'm ready to fight.
The fluffiest pillows, oh what a dream,
Binge-watching shows, it's the perfect scheme.

The dog's on my lap, purring like mad,
With every new scene, I laugh and I'm glad.
Friends on the screen, it feels like a party,
Sharing our jokes, we won't ever be tardy.

So here's to the nights of pure glee,
In a world that's silly, just you and me.
With comfort and joy, we'll conquer the night,
In our cozy kingdom, everything feels right.

The Sound of Laughter

A knock on the door, it's my friend Dave,
With jokes so corny, you know I'll rave.
In the kitchen, we're cooking up fun,
As laughter bounces, we've just begun.

A slip on the floor, he takes a wild dive,
We're rolling with giggles, we're so alive.
"Just a pratfall!" he claims, with flair,
But I see a pastry stuck in his hair!

Board games explode with silly debates,
As we wait for dinner, the timing elates.
Each pun we share, a true masterpiece,
In the art of laughter, there's joy and peace.

So hear my advice, when times get tough,
Just call up a friend, and laugh till it's rough.
For the sound of laughter is truly divine,
It's the best kind of medicine, the perfect wine.

Tales by the Fireside

Gather 'round, let's spin some yarns,
With shadows dancing, we'll bring out the charms.
A story of squirrels with hats and capes,
Who plotted and danced, escaped from their drapes.

The fire crackles, sending sparks high,
A marshmallow toast, oh my, how they fly!
Just one too many, and they all get stuck,
On every old tree, now what's up with that luck?

Uncle Joe tells of his great big catch,
A fish so grand, it put up a match.
But truth be told, it's now just a tale,
And that fish, dear friends? It's now a whale!

So here by the fire, we share a cheer,
Each funny moment, we hold very dear.
With tales of adventure from the past,
In the warmth of the night, friendships will last.

The Gift of Togetherness

In the land of socks where all matches flee,
We gather together, just you and me.
With mismatched patterns, oh what a sight,
This gift of togetherness feels so right.

Our meal's a feast, a culinary mess,
A sprinkle of this, and then too much less.
When cooking together, the kitchen's a blast,
And then we remember, it's joy that will last.

Games on the table, and laughter in the air,
Each silly moment, we happily share.
We trip on our words, but we dance on our feet,
In this circus of life, it's a joyous retreat.

So raise up your glass, here's to the fun,
In the gift of togetherness, we've certainly won.
With love and with laughter, the seasons will flow,
In the warmth of our hearts, let the good times grow.

A Dance of Shadows and Light

In the glow of the moon, the shadows sway,
The cats start a tango, hip-hop ballet.
They twirl and they twist, all through the night,
While we just sit back, giggling with delight.

A lamp flickers on with a jazzy flair,
To join in the fun, it gives a bright glare.
The dog howls a solo, what a strange sight,
In this wacky dance of shadows and light.

The toaster pops up, not wanting to lag,
As crumbs do the cha-cha from out of the bag.
Even the fridge hums a jazzy tune,
As we all laugh, under the silly moon.

So grab your partner, let's not be shy,
In this silly soirée, we'll dance till we cry.
In the chaos we find, laughter takes flight,
In the whimsical world of shadows and light.

Yuletide Whispers in the Air

Santa's got stuck in the chimney again,
We laugh as he wiggles, he's our jolly friend!
The reindeer are munching on snacks by the fire,
While we try to find where those silly lights fliers!

Mistletoe hanging, but who needs that charm?
When hot cocoa spills, it does quite the harm.
Uncle Bob's dancing, a sight to behold,
Spinning like tinsel, but bursting with gold.

The stockings are filled, but who stole the sweets?
The elf in the corner, has sugary feats.
With candy canes flying through the festive night,
We giggle and whisper, it all feels so right.

As snowflakes cascade and we gather around,
The warmth of our laughter is perfectly found.
So, let's raise our cups, to this whimsical flair,
In the joyful echoes of Yuletide air.

Frosty Kisses and Wistful Wishes

The snowman is grinning with buttons of coal,
While frosty kisses take on a happy stroll.
They glide on the ice, twirling with glee,
While we laugh and yell, 'Let's make a snow spree!'

Down the lane, the kids throw snowballs with cheer,
While dogs chase their tails, oh what a dear!
A snow angel makes a wish on the ground,
And giggles and gasps are the happiest sounds.

The hot cocoa bubbles, marshmallows fly,
With each frosty sip, we mention why,
That winter brings dreams wrapped in frosted delight,
With memories made in the chill of the night.

So when the snow falls, let laughter unfurl,
For frosty kisses will brighten this world.
Wistful wishes dance, like snowflakes they play,
In the winter wonderland, joy leads the way.

The Secret Beneath the Mistletoe

Beneath the mistletoe, odd things can occur,
A cat gives a smooch, it's quite the warm blur.
A squirrel steals a kiss, with acorns to spare,
While chickens sing ballads, without a care.

Grandma's sneaky plan with her notorious pie,
She claims if you kiss, you'll never run dry!
So everyone pouts, and looks to their friend,
As the countdown begins, the laughter won't end.

A grumpy old uncle, with lips like a fish,
Whispers his secrets, and grants every wish.
We giggle and snicker, avoiding the trap,
The mistletoe's power is quite the mishap.

So let this fond tale of odd kisses inspire,
To share lots of giggles, and dreams that won't tire.
For in every corner, with laughter we flow,
There's magic and merriment beneath mistletoe.

Heartstrings and Holly

In a quaint little town with a penchant for cheer,
The holly was jolly, but the berries were weird.
One tasted like gravel, the other like coal,
We questioned our choices, and they took quite a toll.

Old Mr. Jenkins with a hat far too tall,
Carried his cat who had claims to the mall.
They danced through the streets like a two-headed show,
We laughed till it hurt, forgetting the snow.

The mistletoe hung with a curious grin,
But it got all our aunts in an awkward spin.
With uncles a-blushing and cousins a-cheer,
We found our heartstrings tied up in the cheer.

As we sipped on hot cocoa, sprinkles galore,
We realized this season had just to explore.
With garlands and giggles, our hearts all took flight,
In the quirky little town, everything felt right.

Starlit Paths to Galaxies

A spaceship made of cheese flew high through the night,
With astronauts wearing pajamas so tight.
They munched on the stars like a cosmic snack,
Curses to gravity, no way to turn back.

Mars wore a tutu, doing a twirl,
While Saturn just laughed, as he gave it a whirl.
The Milky Way danced with a twinkling light,
In a galaxy far, where the laughter took flight.

Space cows floated by, mooing in rhyme,
Cowgirl in PJs, calling it prime time.
They sung country ballads with comets that spin,
And planets that boogied while we all joined in.

As we zoomed through the cosmos with giggles and glee,
We learned that the universe fits on a tree.
So grab a few friends, and let's take a ride,
On starlit paths, where the strange things abide.

The Magic of a Snowy Evening

On a snowy eve with a chill in the air,
We built a snowman with a flair of despair.
His eyes were made of buttons, but they looked quite sad,
Maybe because his carrot nose wasn't rad.

Around him we gathered, in mittens too small,
To share goofy stories and memories that'll brawl.
We each took a turn, telling tales of our fumbles,
The snowman just smiled as he quietly grumbles.

In the moonlight, we roasted marshmallows with glee,
Except Dad caught fire and spilled hot cocoa tea!
With laughter erupting, we gathered around,
Magic found in the warmth, where joy can be found.

As snowflakes kept falling, we tripped and we slid,
On magical evenings, it's the fun that we hid.
With snowmen and laughter, this night was quite bright,
In a snowy embrace, everything felt just right.

Echoes of Laughter in the Chill

In the frost-bitten park, where the wind likes to play,
We gathered together on a chilly fine day.
With snowball fights raging, our cheeks all aglow,
We tickled the air with our laughter and woe.

Old Granny McFluff in a hat far too wide,
Declared she could ski down the hill without pride.
But with one mighty push, she flew like a star,
Landed straight into a snowbank, oops, there went her car!

The sleds were all tangled, a chaotic parade,
As we chased after sleds that were not even made.
Through sticks and through stones, we zigged and we zagged,
While echoes of laughter around us just bragged.

So we'll gather again on those frosty white hills,
In a world full of giggles, far away from the thrills.
With snowmen as allies, and joy as our pill,
In echoes of laughter, our hearts feel the chill.

Heartfelt Greetings

I sent a card with a cat on the front,
It sang a tune while I tried to hunt.
Wishing you smiles, and a pie in the sky,
But I burnt the crust, oh me, oh my!

With hugs and high-fives wrapped in a bow,
My brain is tangled, just so you know.
Keep your socks clean as you jump all around,
In this jolly circus, we've got walls to break down!

Cookies are baking, look out for the smoke,
The dog is now dancing, oh what a joke!
Cheers to the laughter, may it never depart,
Just like my socks, forever playing their part!

Here's to the moments that slip through our hands,
Like glue on a cat—oh, how it expands!
So laugh with abandon, don't take life too keen,
Let's party like penguins in the land of green!

A Sky Lit by Stars

Tonight, the sky looks like spilled confetti,
I saw a comet that looked just unsteady.
Wishing on wishes, how silly we seem,
It's like wishing for cookies while deep in a dream!

The moon's doing yoga, all twisted in light,
It giggles and chuckles, such a curious sight.
Stars twinkle down like cheeky little sprites,
Dancing on rooftops, igniting our nights!

Fireflies joining, a luminous crew,
They wink and they blink, just to confuse you.
Let's gather our dreams and toss them up high,
Like popcorn at movies, let's give it a try!

So under this canvas with stories untold,
Let laughter ring out 'til the night grows old.
Stars whisper secrets that tickle the mind,
In this celestial circus, let's be entwined!

Whispers of Generosity

A cookie for you, and a cupcake for me,
We'll share our dessert like two bees in a tree.
The sprinkle parade is a sugary sight,
But don't eat the strawberry, we might start a fight!

The neighbor's out sharing his funny old hats,
While I'm over here wrestling with twenty-two cats.
Let's spread the good vibes like butter on toast,
And laugh at our blunders, oh, aren't we the most?

From lending a hand to a friend just in need,
To planting a smile—together we'd lead.
We'll dance through the kitchen and twirl with delight,
In the grand game of kindness, we'll both take flight!

So here's to the whispers that carry us near,
With hearts wide open, let's spread some good cheer.
Let laughter resound 'neath the sun and the stars,
For kindness is crazy, just look at our cars!

Festive Spirit and Cheer

The tinsel is tangled, the lights barely blink,
I tripped on the dog—oh, what do you think?
Yet joy reels around like a candy cane twist,
With laughter exploding—can't let it be missed!

We're baking up cookies, but wait, where's the flour?
The cat just ate all of it—oh, what power!
With hats on our heads, we'll sing out of tune,
And dance with the ornaments under the moon!

So raise up your glasses filled with bright cheer,
To friends and to family who bring us near.
May the cookies be crunchy, and the punch have a fizz,
In our wacky winter wonder, we're all in a whiz!

Festive spirits soared, as we try to stay warm,
With cousins and uncles who bring their own charm.
So gather together, let memories grow,
In this jolly ruckus, let's go with the flow!

Underneath the Mistletoe

I stood beneath that mistletoe,
With hopes that you would come and go.
You walked right past, gave me a wink,
And left me there—oh, what to think?

Your lips on someone else's cheek,
While I'm here feeling rather bleak.
Guess my luck's just like a sleigh,
It never comes my way to play!

Tonight I'll pout, then drink some cheer,
And dance alone, no need for fear.
With cookies, milk, and festive cheer,
I'll toast to love that's far and near!

So here's my plan, I've set the stage,
I'll hang a sign: "Come kiss this sage!"
If you still pass me by this time,
I'll just blame it on the silly rhyme.

Wondrous Winter Dreams

The snowflakes twirl, a dance so bright,
I dreamed of sledding through the night.
But then I woke, what a great shock,
My sled was stuck—my favorite block!

The ice was thin, the wind was brash,
I slipped and slid, what a big crash!
With every fall, I'd laugh and cheer,
My winter dreams are filled with cheer!

Hot cocoa spills, the mugs they clink,
My marshmallows swim, I start to think.
That snowman there just gave me a wink,
He knows my plans, I need a drink!

So here's to dreams in frosty air,
Where snowmen dance without a care.
I'll build my dreams, with a warm heart,
And skate away, let winter start!

The Glow of Candlelight

Candlelight flickers, shadows play,
I thought romance would find its way.
But then the cat jumped right on by,
And set my lovely scarf on fire!

I wanted charm, a soft delight,
But now I'm left with quite a fright.
The wax drips down like melting snow,
And I can't find my dinner, oh no!

I dance around, the flames they dance,
Trying hard to salvage a chance.
But light and chaos, what a sight,
I'll laugh it off, just call it night!

So let the candles brightly shine,
With laughter shared and love divine.
Next time I'll use a little care,
I'll keep the cat and flames elsewhere!

Hearts Wrapped in Kindness

Tiny gifts wrapped up with care,
I made them all, a joyful dare.
But when I tried to tie a bow,
I tangled up like it's a show!

The dog went barking, joined the fray,
As ribbons flew in wild display.
My heart wrapped tight, though quite a mess,
Perhaps my gifts need less finesse!

A heart of gold is still the goal,
But with my skills, I lost control.
So with a shrug, I say, "Oh well,"
These gifts of love, they sure still sell!

So here's to hearts wrapped up in cling,
In all our flaws, let kindness sing.
No perfect bows or shiny wrappings,
Just laughter, joy, and happy clappings!

The Glow of Hope

In a world full of worries, we find a light,
A glimmer of laughter, it's quite a sight.
Balloons full of dreams, they float in the air,
As we chase our ambitions, with a quirky flair.

Hopes like rubber ducks, they bounce and they swim,
Twirling and splashing, on a joyous whim.
With each little giggle, the clouds drift away,
We embrace the bright futures that come with the day.

So hold onto that hope, it shines like a star,
Even in darkness, it's never too far.
Just remember to chuckle, let merriment spread,
With laughter as fuel, there's nothing to dread.

For hopes are like cookies, all warm and sweet,
They brighten our days, a delightful treat.
When the glow of hope flickers, just give it a poke,
And watch as it bursts into giggles and smoke.

Wrapped in Warm Wishes

On rainy days perfect for cozying up tight,
Wrap yourself in warm wishes, it's sheer delight.
Like a big fluffy blanket, soft and sincere,
They'll hug you so gently, casting out fear.

With wishes like cookies, all freshly baked,
Each bite is a hug; joy simply can't be faked.
Sprinkled with laughter, and frosted with glee,
Wrapped in warm wishes, just let yourself be.

A wish for your smile, like sun on your face,
A sprinkle of magic, a warm, fuzzy grace.
With friends by your side, you'll feast on good cheer,
And wrap your heart in happiness, year after year.

So toss all your worries and wiggle your toes,
In pajamas and dreams, life's warmth overflows.
Wrapped in these wishes, you'll soar ever high,
Like a kite in the breeze, you'll dance through the sky.

The Language of Love

In the language of love, there's giggles and grins,
A wink from the heart where all joy begins.
With chocolate bar whispers and cupcake delight,
We share silly jokes long into the night.

It's the words without speaking, the smiles that we send,
Like soft fluffy puppies that wag and pretend.
With hugs made of sunshine, and kisses of cake,
Love's language is sweetness, not one word to fake.

With every small gesture, it quietly grows,
Like a garden of daisies, where affection flows.
A tickle, a nudge, or a playful chase,
Can turn any moment into a warm embrace.

So speak it with laughter, let joy be the guide,
Let love be the giggle that bubbles inside.
In this sweet conversation, we'll dance hand in glove,
Finding joy in the words of the language of love.

A Tinsel-Touched Dream

In a tinsel-touched dream, where sparkles reside,
Laughter twirls like ribbons, all fluffy with pride.
With candy cane wishes and snowflakes of cheer,
We'll dance through the night, with friends gathered near.

Mittens made of marshmallows, warmth on our hands,
We'll twirl through the visions of candy land plans.
As cookies and cocoa dance under the moon,
In a tinsel-touched dream, we sing our own tune.

With snowmen that giggle and moonbeams that shine,
Each moment's a treasure, each laugh is divine.
Wrapped in our dreams, we'll hold magic so close,
In a world filled with joy, it's you I love most.

So let's sip on the sweetness, let's spin in delight,
In a tinsel-touched wonder, all cozy and bright.
With laughter as music, our hearts become free,
In this dream wrapped in tinsel, it's bliss, can't you see?

The Spirit of Giving

With a ribbon and bow, you're ready to go,
But what's in the box? It's a big surprise, you know!
A sweater two sizes too big for Uncle Lou,
He'll wear it with pride, or maybe as a shoe.

Neighbors bring treats, we all start to munch,
A fruitcake that's older than my Aunt's pet crunch.
We gather and laugh, it's the highlight of the night,
As we gift-wrap the cat, to everyone's delight.

The spirit of giving is a wacky affair,
From vacuuming dust bunnies to combing the hair.
Each gift tells a story, each card brings a grin,
Except the one from Grandma - it's just a used tin!

So raise up your mugs and toast with good cheer,
For the awkward traditions that bring us all near.
In the end, we'll remember, through giggles and grins,
The joy of the season, where silliness wins!

Evergreen Blessings

In the corner stands a tree, so proud and tall,
Decked with shiny baubles, it could outshine them all.
But when the cat leaps up, to snag just one thing,
A cascade of ornaments - oh what a fling!

Lights twinkle and flash, like stars in the night,
But one bulb is broken - oh, what a fright!
The tree leans a bit, as if it needs a drink,
Maybe it's the eggnog, or just my own wink.

Evergreen blessings fill up the room,
As we all dance around – oh, smell that perfume!
But hidden in the branches, what could it be?
A whole stash of cookies - for you, not for me!

So let's cherish this moment, with laughter and cheer,
With family and friends, and a pinch of good beer.
For amidst the chaos, the mess that it brings,
Are evergreen blessings, and the joy that it sings!

Joyful Gatherings

We gather around, in our festive best clothes,
Some sport a big sweater, with reindeer and bows.
The turkey is burnt, it looks like a prank,
But laughter is better than giving thanks to the tank!

The table is set with food piled up high,
From mashed potatoes to pie - oh my, oh my!
Yet Uncle Fred whispers, with a half-chewed bite,
"Did anyone order the fruitcake tonight?"

With toasts that go wrong, and games that misfire,
Someone will fall in the hot Christmas fire.
Yet still we all cheer, for the joy that we share,
For family and friends, there's love everywhere!

So here's to the gatherings that come every year,
With laughter and chaos, let's all raise a cheer!
For in the end, it's the fun we all find,
That keeps us together - and silly in kind!

The Aroma of Cinnamon

The oven is humming, something's afoot,
The aroma of cinnamon, oh how we hoot!
Baking cookies and cakes, with sprinkles and flair,
But what's with the brown stuff that sticks to your hair?

The dough sticks together like glue on your hands,
Trying to measure, but nothing expands.
A pinch of this, a scoop of that,
What's that, Auntie? Is that a cat?

With ribbons and frosting, we're ready to bake,
But here comes the dog, oh what a mistake!
He snags a whole cookie, with a cheeky grin,
And now he stands guard, that gluttonous kin.

So we laugh and we roll, through the hot, sweet haze,
Celebrating with sprinkles and buttery bays.
The aroma of cinnamon fills up the air,
In this kitchen of chaos, there's love everywhere!

The Frosted Hearth

The firewood's stacked, but where's the match?
I've looked all over, in every patch.
Burning fluff would surely be a treat,
But it might just roast my favorite seat.

The cat's on the rug, in a sunbeam sunbathing,
While I'm left here, my plans degrading.
The cocoa's cold, as it sits on the shelf,
Maybe I should just warm it up myself.

Around the hearth, there's laughter and cheer,
As Uncle Joe recounts tales from last year.
But the stories grow taller, and funnier, too,
I think he just might have made that one stew!

So gather 'round, let's share a toast,
For frosted hearths and the friends we love most!
But remember to keep the marshmallows near,
Trusted outsiders—they bring us all cheer.

Jingle Bells and Joyful Hearts

Jingle bells ringing, but where's my hat?
I've lost it again, and my shoes look like that.
With a scarf made of tinsel, I strut on the street,
Hoping the neighbors won't think I'm a treat.

Joyful hearts pounding, I've got moves to show,
Dancing in the snow like a pro—rather slow.
I slipped on a patch, doing spins like a top,
And now all the kids have gathered to stop.

A snowman is born, with a carrot for a nose,
But who knew his three buttons would pose?
He wobbles in laughter, his arms in the air,
While I'm busy wondering how I got here, I swear.

So let's keep on jingling, with joy in our soul,
Our holiday spirit spins out of control.
Cue the cocoa, with marshmallows bold,
It's the laughter and warmth that never grows old.

Enchanted Snowflakes

Look at the snowflakes, so shiny and bright,
They fall from the sky, giving us quite a fright.
Each one's a treasure, unique they do land,
Except for the one that lands in my hand.

They tickle my nose, and oh how they fly,
I'm dodging and weaving, oh my, oh my!
A dance with the snowflakes, a chilly romance,
But losing my balance? Now that's not my chance.

They twirl and they whirl, a magical sight,
But my gloves are so wet; this isn't quite right.
I'm getting all soggy; it's cold as a shock,
As I trip on my laces and directly hit the block.

So here's to the snowflakes, both laugh and delight,
For a world filled with whimsy, so merry and bright.
Let's plan a retreat, have fun in the freeze,
Just remember to wear socks, and bring snacks to tease!

A Time for Giving

It's that time of year when we share and we care,
But whose turn is it? I can't find the chair!
Gifts piled so high, like a mountain up high,
I'm just hoping the dog won't give them a try.

My holiday spirit's shining so bright,
Wrapped in a bow, tucked away out of sight.
But each time I peek for a little surprise,
It's just Aunt Mabel's old plaid suit (oh my eyes!).

Tinsel and garland are draped everywhere,
As we trip on the lights while searching for flair.
But laughter and joy are the best gifts of all,
Even if they come wrapped in a rogue snowball.

So here's to the joy that we share every year,
For the moments we treasure, the people we cheer.
Let's toast to the mishaps that make it just right,
And remember that love's the best gift—what a delight!

A Tapestry of Traditions

In winter coats, we trudge through snow,
Hoping to find where the hot cocoa flows.
A dance with the dog, what a sight to behold,
He swipes the snacks, oh, he's bold and uncontrolled.

Grandma's in the kitchen, oh what a scene,
Burnt the turkey? Nah, it's all just cuisine!
We laugh and we sing, as the fire pops bright,
Wearing socks on our hands, who needs gloves tonight?

Bright Eyes and Full Hearts

With cookies so big, we can't even share,
Each crumb that falls leads to laughter and flair.
Pajama parties where mischief holds reign,
We'll prank the cat, oh the chaos and gain!

Sipping our punch from a bowl made of fruit,
Someone slipped a pickle – oh, what a hoot!
A toast to the folks with their sparkling cheer,
May their jokes be as funny as last year's reindeer.

Glimmering Ornaments

The tree is a sight, with baubles galore,
One cat attempts climbing, what's in store?
Tinsel and glitter now cover the floor,
Is it decor or a sparkly war?

In matching sweaters, we're a sight to see,
One sparkly snowman has the audacity.
We giggle and grin, our hearts all aglow,
While Uncle Joe's dancing? Oh, just let it go!

Echoes of Love

Gather 'round while I tell you a tale,
Of mischief and love that will never grow stale.
There's cousin who sings, but off-key, oh dear,
Yet we all clap loud, for the love that we cheer.

With each silly story, we water the roots,
Of memories made in our festive pursuits.
So here's to our family, crazy and loud,
With hearts intertwined, we are forever proud.

Winter's Embrace

Snowflakes dance like silly clowns,
Making white coats on sleepy towns.
Frosty breath in the air we share,
Icicles hang without a care.

Hot cocoa in my frozen hands,
As snowmen plot their snowball bands.
Sledding down the hill with glee,
Oh look! I've landed in a tree!

Mittens misplaced, where could they be?
Oh dear, now my fingers freeze!
Winter's chill, a frosty tease,
Wrapped in layers, oh such ease!

Laughing at the slip and slide,
Grumpy faces trying to hide.
Yet through it all, we share this cheer,
Winter's magic, oh so dear!

The Joy of Giving

Wrapping gifts with tape and flair,
Mom's old socks, a present rare!
Tangled bows, a funny sight,
I gift you socks, oh pure delight!

Christmas cards, a printed face,
In every box, a silly grace.
I'm not sure how you'll react,
But laughter's what I hope you'll pack!

Cookies made with love and cheer,
Burned on tops, but taste is clear.
A plate of joy, that's what I pray,
Munching crumbs through Christmas day!

So as we cheer, let's share the fun,
Gifting humor, one by one.
For in the joy of what we share,
The laughter inside, we can't compare!

A Season of Reflection

Looking back at all my blunders,
Like wearing socks in summer thunder.
Thoughts of past, they dance around,
Oh, the goofy moments found!

I tripped last year on holiday cheer,
Spilled the punch, oh my, oh dear!
But through those slips, I've gained some grace,
With laughter lines upon my face.

Reflecting on the joy we've made,
From burnt dinners to games we played.
Memories brought together tight,
In every giggle, pure delight.

So raise your glass; we've come so far,
Together underneath the stars.
In this season of reflection,
Let's toast to laughs and sweet affection!

Holiday Hues of Happiness

Lights are strung like tangled hair,
Colors flashing everywhere.
Red and green, a quirky spree,
Dance of hues all around me!

Ornaments that make you laugh,
One-eyed Santa, a silly gaffe.
Stockings hung a bit askew,
The cat's climbed in—what will we do?

Mistletoe hung with crafty flair,
"Oops!" I said; I'm stuck in there!
Silly kisses that make us cringe,
Holiday fun on the edge of a binge!

Through every shade and holiday cheer,
Let's celebrate with loved ones near.
For in the hues of warmth and grace,
Happy holidays fill every space!

The Celebration of Togetherness

In a room filled with laughter, we dance and we sway,
With my socks on the carpet, I slip and I play.
Family and friends, we gather in cheer,
Someone brings cake—oh dear, it's nearly gone, I fear!

Raise a glass to the mishaps, the bloopers, the fun,
Remember that time when we jumped and we spun?
Our jokes may be silly, our stories a mess,
But together we're happy, I must confess!

Bottled up bickering from last New Year's feast,
Is lost in the giggles and jokes that won't cease.
We toast to the memories we share all around,
And nobody notices who's still half-way down!

So here's to togetherness, the joy that we find,
May our laughter ring out, and our hearts be aligned.
With friends by our side, let's dance one more time,
And unless you are my twin, don't steal my last lime!

Splendors of the Season

Winter brings snowflakes, all fluffy and white,
I slip on the ice and that's not quite right.
With mittens and scarves wrapped up snug on my nose,
I smile through the shivers, till my hot chocolate glows.

Springtime bursts forth with a rainbow of blooms,
But my allergies come—send me straight to the rooms!
With pollen in the air, I sneeze and I wheeze,
While flowers attract bees that buzz like a tease.

Summer's a scorcher, the sun's blazing bright,
Jump in the pool, where it's cool and just right.
But then comes the tan lines, a sight to behold,
I'm striped like a zebra—such stories I've told!

Autumn arrives with its colorful leaves,
But come rake up the yard, and oh how it deceives!
A pile that looks lovely soon scatters away,
As the wind sends my labor on a raucous ballet!

The Fire's Soft Glow

Gather 'round the fire, let's share tales tonight,
As the marshmallows toast to a delicious delight.
I brought the guitar, but don't run away,
My singing's like sweetness—just a bit by the way!

The fire's glow dances, it flickers and sways,
And shadows start forming, in peculiar ways.
What's that by the log? Oh wait, that's my shoe!
Just don't tell the bears I'm here, or they'll come too!

We roast up the s'mores, as the stars fill the sky,
With laughter and giggles, we let all worries fly.
And if your hair's smoky, it's just part of the game,
You'll smell like a campfire, but don't you feel lame!

As the night wraps around us, the fire's nearly spent,
We'll promise to gather again, oh, it's heaven-sent!
So let's raise our mugs, full of cocoa and cheer,
And toast to the memories we create every year!

The Warmth of Kindness

There's magic in kindness, like a hug that's so tight,
It chases the shadows and fills hearts with light.
A smile is contagious, just watch how it spreads,
Like butter on toast; it's good for our heads!

When something goes wrong, and the road gets quite tough,
Don't fear, here's a cupcake—oh, I hope they're enough!
A little bit of laughter, a sprinkle of care,
Can turn any frown into smiles everywhere.

From helping a stranger with bags made of gold,
To sharing your lunch when they're feeling quite cold.
Kindness brings warmth, like a hug from a friend,
It's the best little gift that we have to send!

So sprinkle your kindness, let it fly through the air,
It'll come back to you, so spread it if you dare!
For in this big world, we're all in the race,
Let's all be the reason someone smiles today—just in case!

Milton Keynes UK
Ingram Content Group UK Ltd.
UKHW022123091224
452185UK00010B/468